CHARTING the COURSE

Book 1
Grade 2-2.5

🎵 Six Charts for Small Jazz Groups

💡 Flexible Instrumentation

🛠 12 Transcribed Solos

🎖 12 Suggested Solos

🎧 49 Play-Along Tracks

Books Available for: **C, B♭, E♭, F, Bass Clef, Tuba, Piano, Vibes/Guitar, Bass, Drums, Score**

© 2016 HXmusic LLC. Produced by Ryan Fraley.

PO Box 206
8206 Rockville Road
Indianapolis, IN 46214
www.ryanfraley.com

Table of Contents

Range Guide

Two versions of **Part 2** are included in each wind book to provide more instrumentation options.
Optional Tuba book doubles Bass. Mallets play from Guitar / Vibes book.

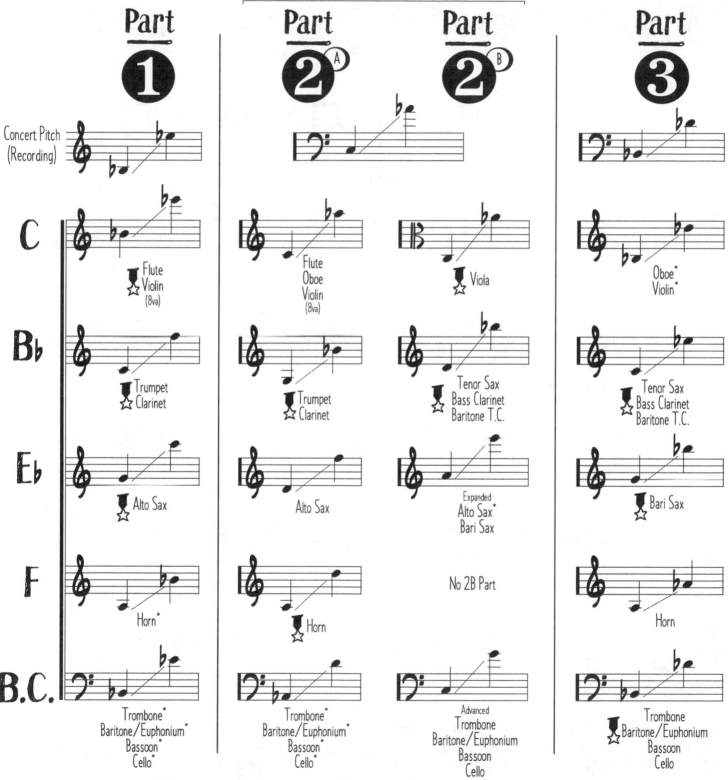

* These parts may be in a different octave than recorded. If possible, avoid them in an ensemble setting.

♩ = Best choice for balance and comfortable ranges.

PORTO ALEGRE

Bb

Trumpet
Clarinet

Part 1

Ryan Fraley
(ASCAP)

Samba (♩=100)

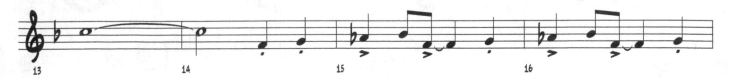

4

6

Porto Alegre

PORTO ALEGRE

Ryan Fraley
(ASCAP)

Bb
Tenor Sax
Bass Clarinet
Baritone T.C.

Part 2 B

Samba (♩ =100)

Porto Alegre

PORTO ALEGRE

Ryan Fraley
(ASCAP)

Bb
Tenor Sax
Bass Clarinet
Baritone T.C.

Part **3**

Samba (♩=100)

10

Porto Alegre

Chords

⇜ Porto Alegre ⇝

Scales

o = Emphasize this note.   x = Don't emphasize this note.

Bb

Porto Alegre
Solo Transcription
as played by Alex Noppe (Trumpet)

Porto Alegre
Suggested Solo

based on Alex Noppe's solo (Trumpet)

Solo Transcription

⇟ Porto Alegre ⇟

as played by Ryan Fraley (Trombone)

♫ Porto Alegre ♫
Suggested Solo

based on Ryan Fraley's solo (Trombone)

18

TIME WILL TELL

Bb
Trumpet
Clarinet
Part 2

Ryan Fraley
(ASCAP)

20

Time Will Tell

22

TIME WILL TELL

Bb
Tenor Sax
Bass Clarinet
Baritone T.C.

Ryan Fraley
(ASCAP)

Part 3

Ballad (Swing) (♩ = 90)

≈ Time Will Tell ≈

Chords

Scales

o = Emphasize this note.   *✗* = Don't emphasize this note.

Time Will Tell
Solo Transcription

as played by Sylvain Carton (Alto Sax)

⇒ Time Will Tell ⇐
Suggested Solo

based on Sylvain Carton's solo (Alto Sax)

B♭

⇜ Time Will Tell ⇝
Solo Transcription
as played by Ryan Fraley (Trombone)

Time Will Tell
Suggested Solo

based on Ryan Fraley's solo (Trombone)

LEAP DAY

B♭

Trumpet
Clarinet

Ryan Fraley
(ASCAP)

Part 1

Swing (♩=132)

LEAP DAY

LEAP DAY

Ryan Fraley
(ASCAP)

⁓ Leap Day ⁓

LEAP DAY

Bb

Tenor Sax
Bass Clarinet
Baritone T.C.

Part 3

Ryan Fraley
(ASCAP)

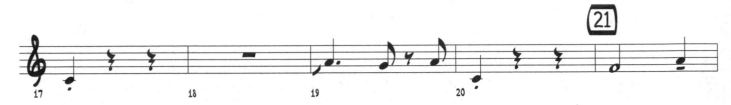

38

Leap Day

⇨ Leap Day ⇦
Chords

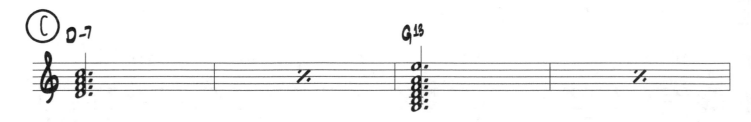

⇟ Leap Day ⇞

Scales

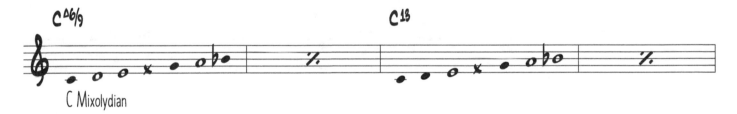

o = Emphasize this note.   x = Don't emphasize this note.

Bb

⇴ Leap Day ⇴
Solo Transcription
as played by Alex Noppe (Trumpet)

(A) C△6/9 ... F7

C7

(B) F7

C△6/9 ... C13

(C) D-7 ... G13

C△6/9 ... A7 ... D-7 ... G+7

Leap Day
Suggested Solo

based on Alex Noppe's solo (Trumpet)

Bb

⸎ Leap Day ⸎
Solo Transcription
as played by Sylvain Carton (Tenor Sax)

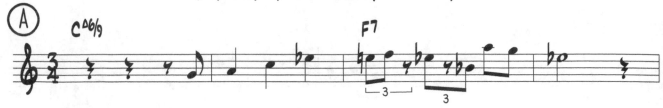

❧ Leap Day ❧
Suggested Solo

based on Sylvain Carton's solo (Tenor Sax)

BOHEMIAN GROOVE

Bb
Trumpet
Clarinet

Ryan Fraley
(ASCAP)

Part 1

Mellow Rock (♩ = 92)

46

Bohemian Groove

BOHEMIAN GROOVE

Bb
Trumpet
Clarinet
Part 2

Ryan Fraley
(ASCAP)

Mellow Rock (♩ = 92)

48

Bohemian Groove

BOHEMIAN GROOVE

Bb
Tenor Sax
Bass Clarinet
Baritone T.C.

Part
2 B

Ryan Fraley
(ASCAP)

Mellow Rock (♩ = 92)

50

Bohemian Groove

BOHEMIAN GROOVE

Ryan Fraley
(ASCAP)

Mellow Rock (♩ = 92)

Bohemian Groove

‑ Bohemian Groove ‑

Chords

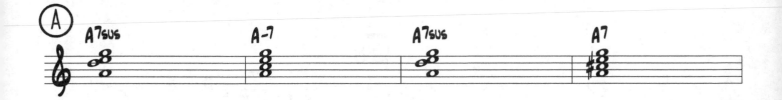

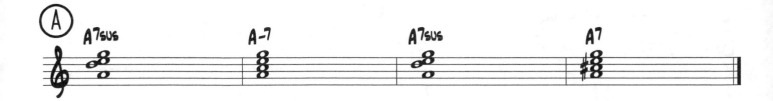

Bohemian Groove

Scales

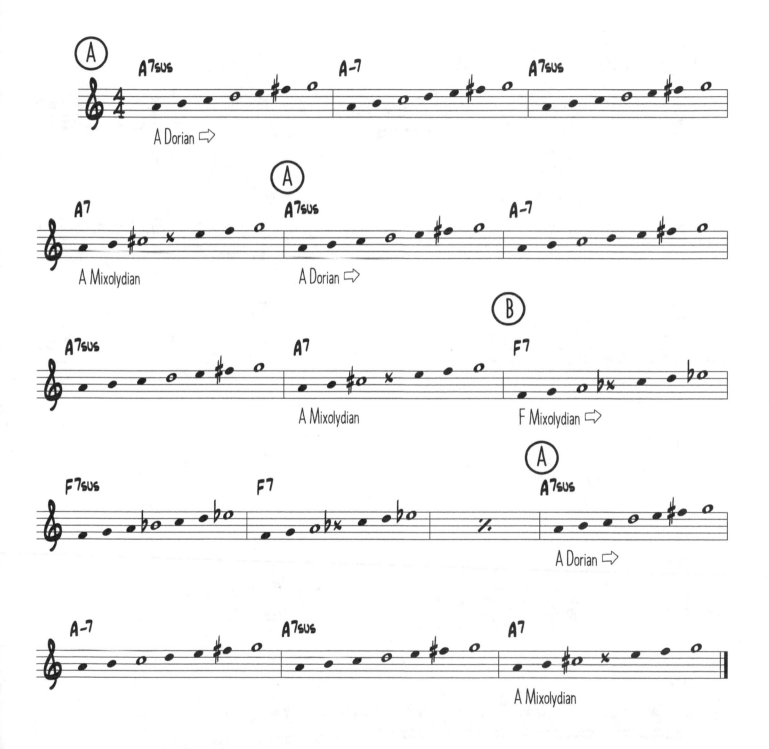

o = Emphasize this note.   x = Don't emphasize this note.

Bᵇ

꙳ Bohemian Groove ꙳
Solo Transcription
as played by Ryan Fraley (Trombone)

Suggested Solo

~ Bohemian Groove ~

based on Ryan Fraley's solo (Trombone)

Bb

Bohemian Groove
Solo Transcription

as played by Bobby Kokinos (Bass)

Solo is transposed 8VA

❧ Bohemian Groove ❧

Suggested Solo

based on Bobby Kokinos's solo (Bass)

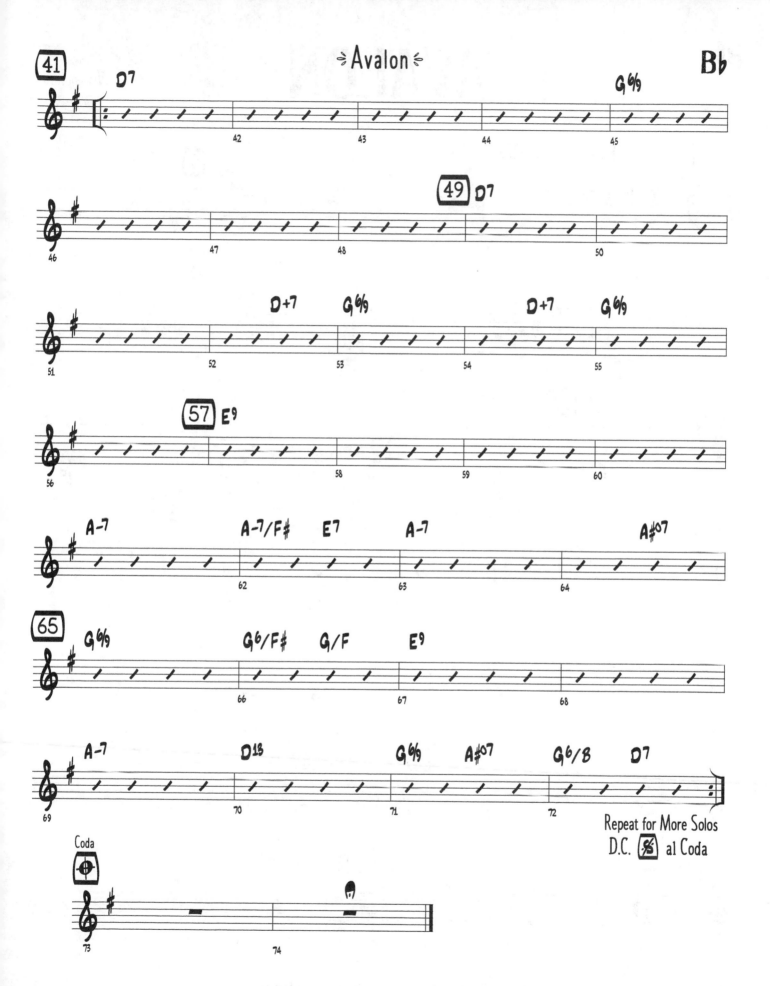

AVALON

Bb

Trumpet
Clarinet

Part 2 A

music by
Vincent Rose

arranged by
Ryan Fraley
(ASCAP)

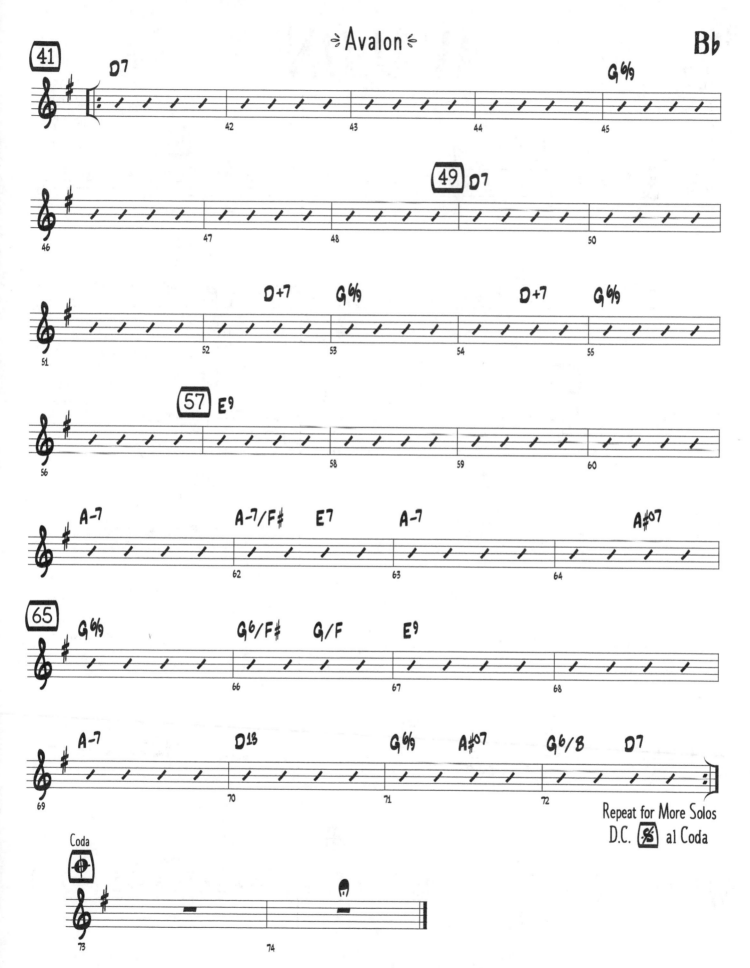

AVALON

music by
Vincent Rose

arranged by
Ryan Fraley
(ASCAP)

Bb
Tenor Sax
Bass Clarinet
Baritone T.C.

Part 2

⋟Avalon⋟

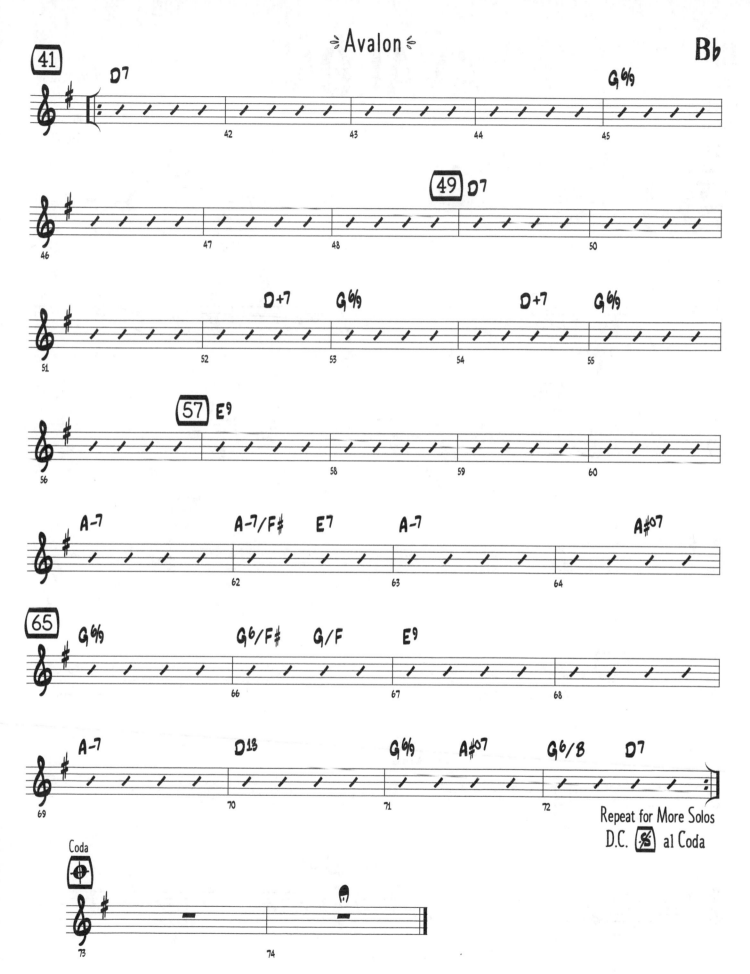

Repeat for More Solos
D.C. 𝄋 al Coda

Avalon

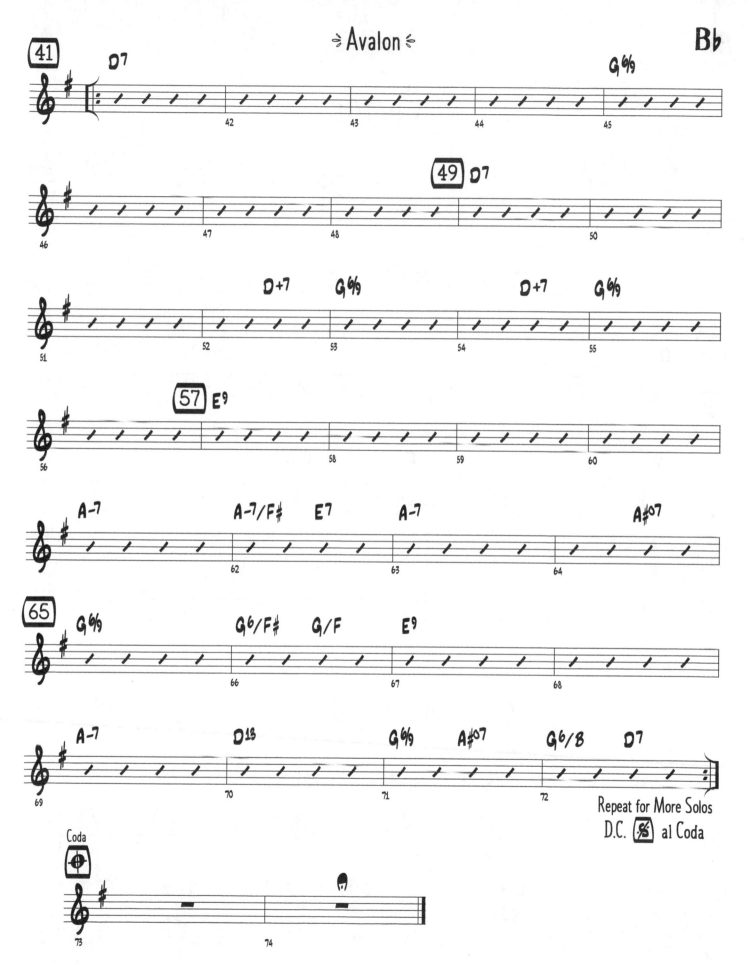

Repeat for More Solos
D.C. 𝄋 al Coda

⇨ Avalon ⇦

Chords

ᚏ Avalon ᚏ

Scales

o = Emphasize this note.   x = Don't emphasize this note.

Avalon
Solo Transcription

as played by Robert Stright (Vibraphone)

Avalon
Suggested Solo
based on Robert Stright's solo (Vibraphone)

Bb

⇜ Avalon ⇝
Solo Transcription

as played by Alex Noppe (Trumpet)

⇘Avalon⇚
Suggested Solo

based on Alex Noppe's solo (Trumpet)

B♭

Trumpet
Clarinet

STEAM PUNK FUNK

Ryan Fraley
(ASCAP)

Part 1

Funky Swing Half-Time Feel (♩=168)

⁌ Steam Punk Funk ⁌

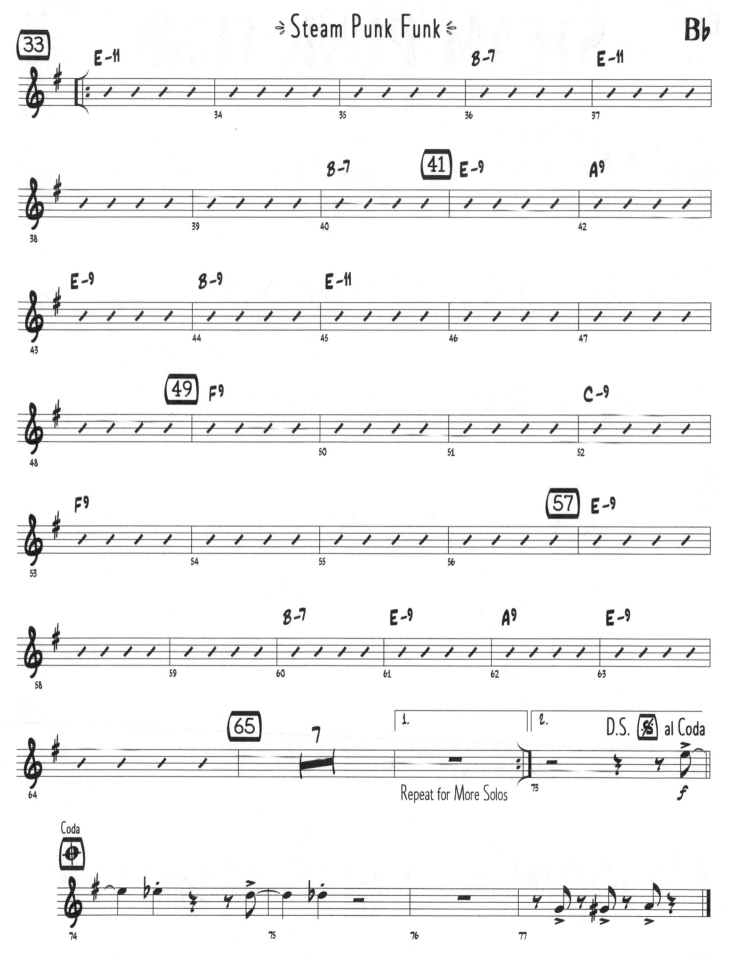

Repeat for More Solos

STEAM PUNK FUNK

Bb

Trumpet
Clarinet

Part 2

Ryan Fraley
(ASCAP)

Funky Swing Half-Time Feel (♩=168)

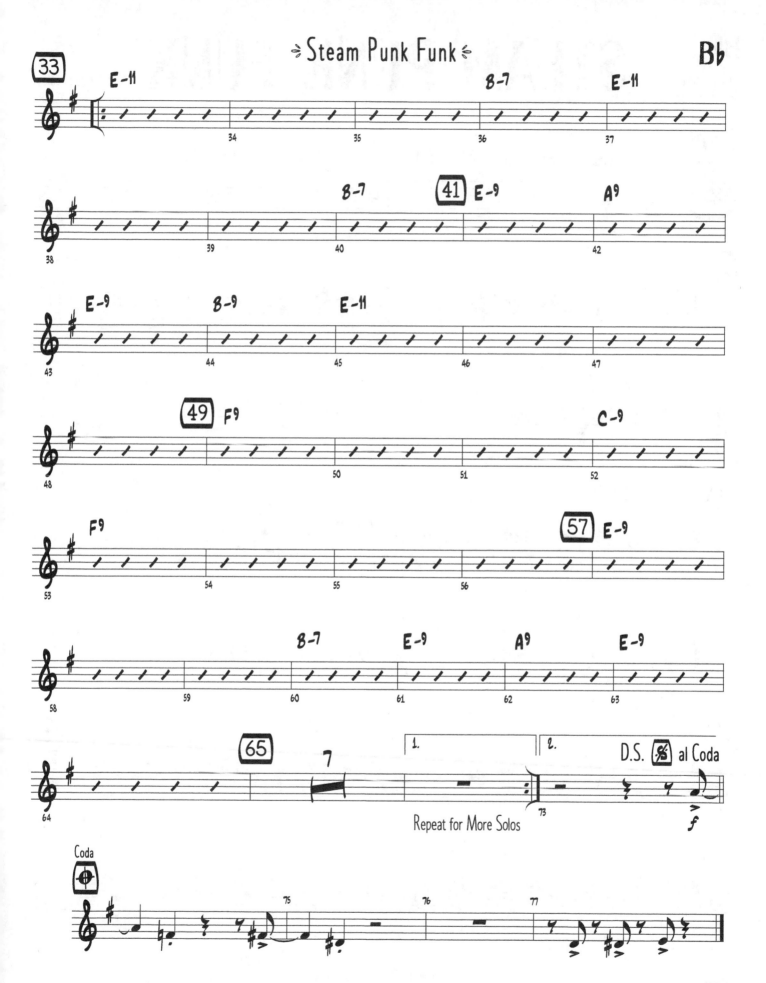

STEAM PUNK FUNK

Ryan Fraley (ASCAP)

Bb
Tenor Sax
Bass Clarinet
Baritone T.C.

Part **2**

78

⤳ Steam Punk Funk ⤳

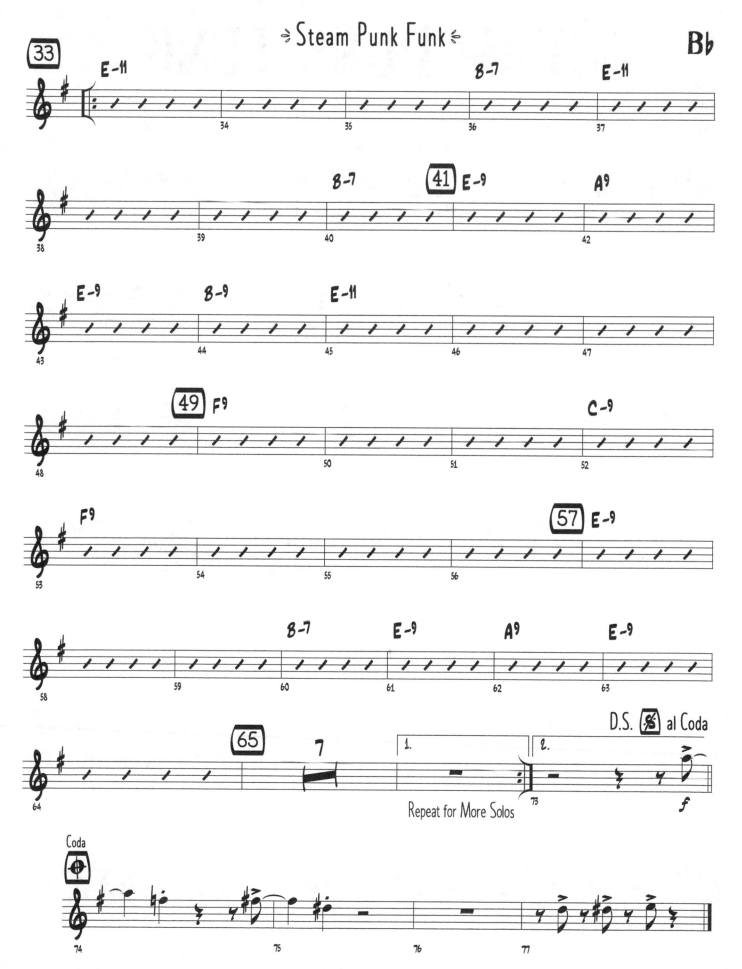

STEAM PUNK FUNK

Bb
Tenor Sax
Bass Clarinet
Baritone T.C.

Part 3

Ryan Fraley
(ASCAP)

Funky Swing Half-Time Feel (♩=168)

To Coda

Steam Punk Funk

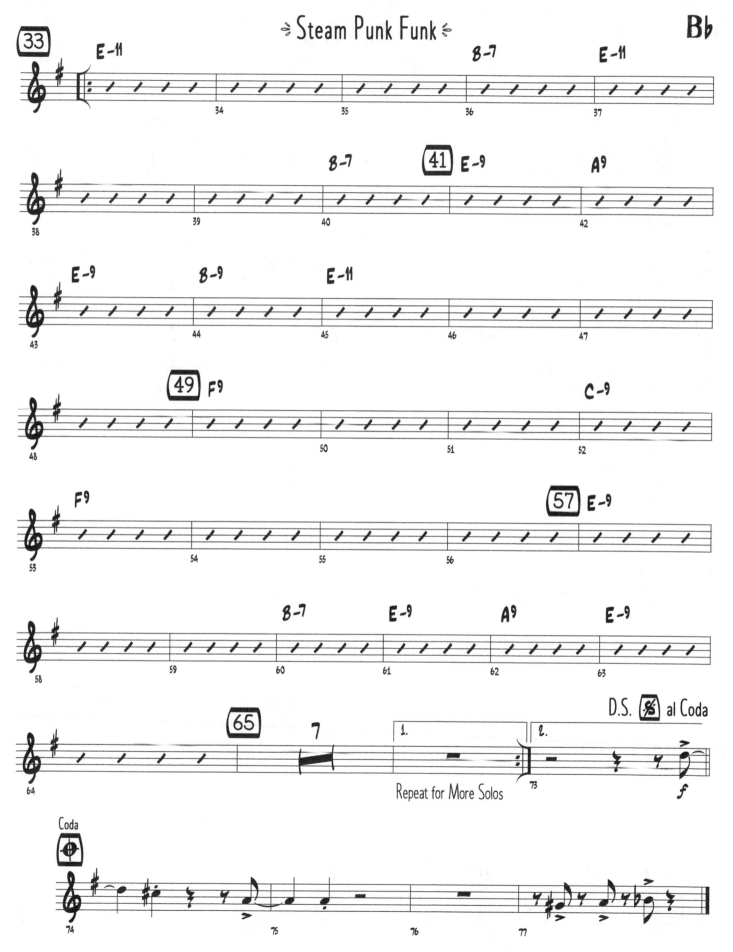

Bb

≈ Steam Punk Funk ≈

Chords

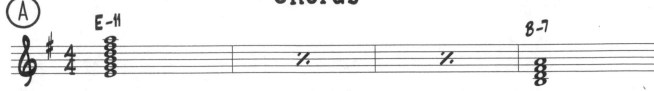

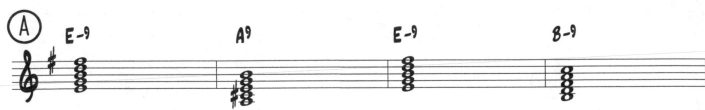

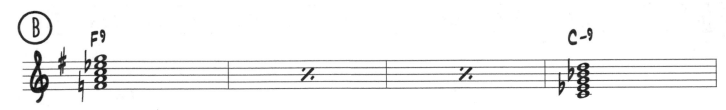

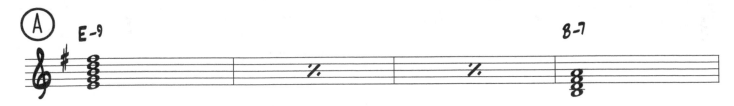

⇌ Steam Punk Funk ⇌
Scales

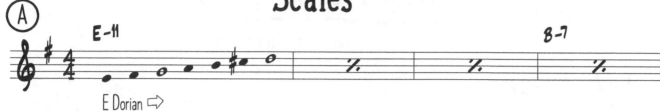

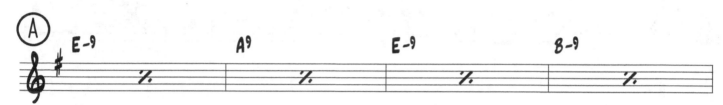

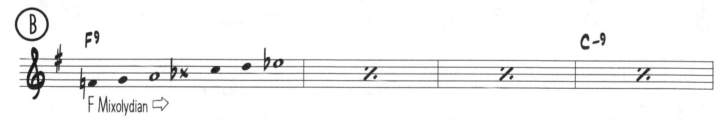

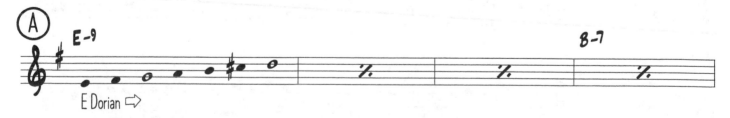

𝑜 = Emphasize this note.   **✗** = Don't emphasize this note.

Steam Punk Funk
Solo Transcription
as played by Sylvain Carton (Tenor Sax)

Bb

⇥ Steam Punk Funk ⇤
Suggested Solo

based on Sylvain Carton's solo (Tenor Sax)

B♭

Bb

⇒ Steam Punk Funk ⇐
Solo Transcription

as played by Isaac Helbling (Guitar)

⇻ Steam Punk Funk ⇺
Suggested Solo

based on Isaac Helbling's solo (Guitar)

About the Soloists

Originally from France, **Sylvain Carton** is a multi-instrumentalist and composer currently residing in Los Angeles. An accomplished saxophonist and guitarist, Sylvain tours and records regularly with a number of groups representing a variety of musical genres and traditions, such as Beats Antique, The Japonize Elephants, The Mitch Marcus Quintet, Aphrodesia, Space Blaster, Khi Darag, Lord Loves a Working Man, John Vanderslice, Maureen and the Mercury Five, Carolyna Picknick, and The Sylvain Carton Quartet.

As a composer, Carton writes extensively for The Japonize Elephants, an eclectic ensemble of seven to twelve musicians playing vibes, violin, bass, guitar, banjo, accordion, junk percussion, trumpet, flute, and saxophones, who like to refer to their music as cinematic old-time eastern honk orchestral music. He also writes extensively for his own jazz quartet in addition to the Mitch Marcus Quintet, the MMQ + 13 big band, Carolyna Picknick, and the 12-piece afro-funk ensemble Aphrodesia. His compositions for big band won a "Subito" grant from the American Composer's Forum. Sylvain has also composed chamber music for small orchestra, string quartet, brass quintet, saxophone quartet, solo pieces for voice, tuba, cello, guitar, saxophone, and clarinet, and has been commissioned to write music for a documentary aired on PBS, several independent films, and Oakland's 'Counterpointe' dance company.

Sylvain Carton holds a BM in Jazz Performance from the Indiana University School of Music at Bloomington, where he studied with David Baker, Eugene Rousseau, Tom Walsh, and Shirley Diamond, as well as an M.A. in music composition from UC Santa Cruz, where he co-directed the Latin American Music Ensemble.

In addition to performing and composing, Sylvain is a Vandoren Performing Artist and Artistic Advisor.

Alex Noppe is the Director of Jazz Studies and Assistant Professor of Trumpet at Boise State University. He has performed as both a classical and jazz musician with ensembles across the country, including the Charlotte Symphony, Indianapolis Chamber Orchestra, Boise Philharmonic, Hal Leonard Jazz Orchestra, and David Baker Big Band. He tours regularly with the Louis Romanos Quartet, recently performing in Hawaii, New Orleans, Salt Lake City, San Francisco, and Atlanta, and can be heard on the group's critically acclaimed release Take Me There. In addition to being a founding member, Noppe is the resident composer/arranger for the Mirari Brass Quintet, which performs numerous concerts each year to audiences across the United States. He has appeared on stage alongside Eric Alexander, Chris Potter, David Liebman, Hank Jones, Wycliffe Gordon, the Count Basie Orchestra, Sylvia McNair, Byron Stripling, John Clayton, Leonard Slatkin, and Garrison Keillor. Noppe has degrees from Indiana University and the University of Michigan, and has composed numerous works for brass quintet and jazz ensemble.

Alex Noppe is an Endorsing Artist for Bach Trumpets.

Ryan Fraley's compositions and arrangements have been performed worldwide by jazz ensembles, orchestras, and bands of all levels. He is the co-founder of Wave Mechanics Union, a studio jazz orchestra with two albums released. The most recent album, *Further to Fly*, was named by College Music Journal as one of the top 50 jazz albums of 2013, based on radio plays. Ryan has provided orchestrations for Jon Anderson (vocalist from the band Yes) for various solo projects, and is a frequent recipient of ASCAP Plus Awards. His commissioned music has appeared in films, albums, commercials, and other media.

Fraley holds a master's degree in music composition from the State University of New York at Potsdam, and a bachelor's degree in music theory and composition from Ball State University.

Robert Stright is a "brilliant, original vibist" according to Harvey Pekar of *Jazziz Magazine*. Robert performs regularly throughout Indiana on vibes, as well as piano, voice and drums. Dr. Stright (DMA, University of Wisconsin-Madison) has taught at Butler University, Purdue University, and Indiana University, and his award-winning compositions are published by Ludwig Music.

Isaac Helbling is a multi-instrumentalist & vocalist, producer, composer, and recording engineer based in the Midwest. He provides engineering, mixing, and mastering services through Blast Doors Audio.

Bobby Kokinos is an active electric and upright bassist in Indiana who has been playing for over 20 years. He has appeared on numerous recordings and has performed along side of some of the area's top musicians. He received a bachelor's degree from Ball State University along with a minor in music performance. Bobby can be seen performing frequently with several of Indy's top jazz and blues ensembles.

Thank you: Abigail Fraley, Vincent Laine, James Grant, Gabriel Harley, Peter Sampson, Bart Roberts, William Frazier, Josh Weirich, Chris Murray, Chris Drabyn, Michael Graham, Dave Olsen, Chaim Rubinov, Philip Groeber, Antonio Ferranti, and of course Sylvain, Alex, Robert, Isaac, and Bobby.

Play-Along Tracks

For each tune, there are play-along tracks available for every instrument part. In addition to the full mixes, you'll find rhythm section-only versions, and tracks that let you sit in with the band as Part 1, Part 2, Part 3, Piano/Guitar/Vibes, Bass, or Drums.

All 49 play-along tracks are discoverable on your favorite music streaming service, or directly below. Find them now at these locations. Search for "**Charting the Course, Vol. 1**".

and more.

Or, just scan this QR Code with your smart phone to access the MP3 files directly. Stream in place or download, burn, & share if you wish.

www.ryanfraley.com